TECHNOLOGIES THAT CHANGED THE WORLD

DRONES

JIM WHITING

JAICO PUBLISHING HOUSE

Ahmedabad Bangalore Chennai
Delhi Hyderabad Kolkata Mumbai

Published by Jaico Publishing House
A-2 Jash Chambers, 7-A Sir Phirozshah Mehta Road
Fort, Mumbai - 400 001
jaicopub@jaicobooks.com
www.jaicobooks.com

Published in arrangement with
The Creative Company
2140 Howard Drive West, North Mankato, MN 56003, USA

To be sold only in India, Bangladesh, Bhutan,
Pakistan, Nepal, Sri Lanka and the Maldives.

Photographs by Alamy (508 collection, imageBROKER), Creative Commons Wikimedia (Dickenson V. Alley, Frank Carter/U.S. Air Force/DVIDS, David Conover/Yank, the Army Weekly/U.S. Army, Photographer's Mate 2nd Class James Elliott/U.S. Navy, Sgt. 1st Class Michael Guillory/U.S. Army, Library of Congress Prints & Photographs Division/ID hec.25529, Tonnelé and Co.), Getty Images (STEPHANIE AGLIETTI/Stringer/AFP, Petri Artturi Asikainen/Taxi, David Bathgate/Corbis Historical, Frederick M. Brown/Stringer/Getty Images Entertainment, Matteo Colombo/Moment, Westend61, Yagi Studio/DigitalVision), iStockphoto (3dts, brunocoelhopt, Joel Carillet, danku, HannesEichinger, richard johnson, kalasek, martin-dm, Onfokus, oticki, Smederevac, Tlillico), Shutterstock (Nesterenko Maxym)

DRONES
ISBN 978-93-90166-96-1

First Jaico Impression: 2023

Page design and layout by
Special Effects Graphics Design Company, Mumbai

Printed by
Trinity Academy For Corporate Training Limited, Mumbai

Contents

Introduction

As drone technology has developed, drones have taken on a wider range of jobs, including launching missiles and monitoring effects of climate change.

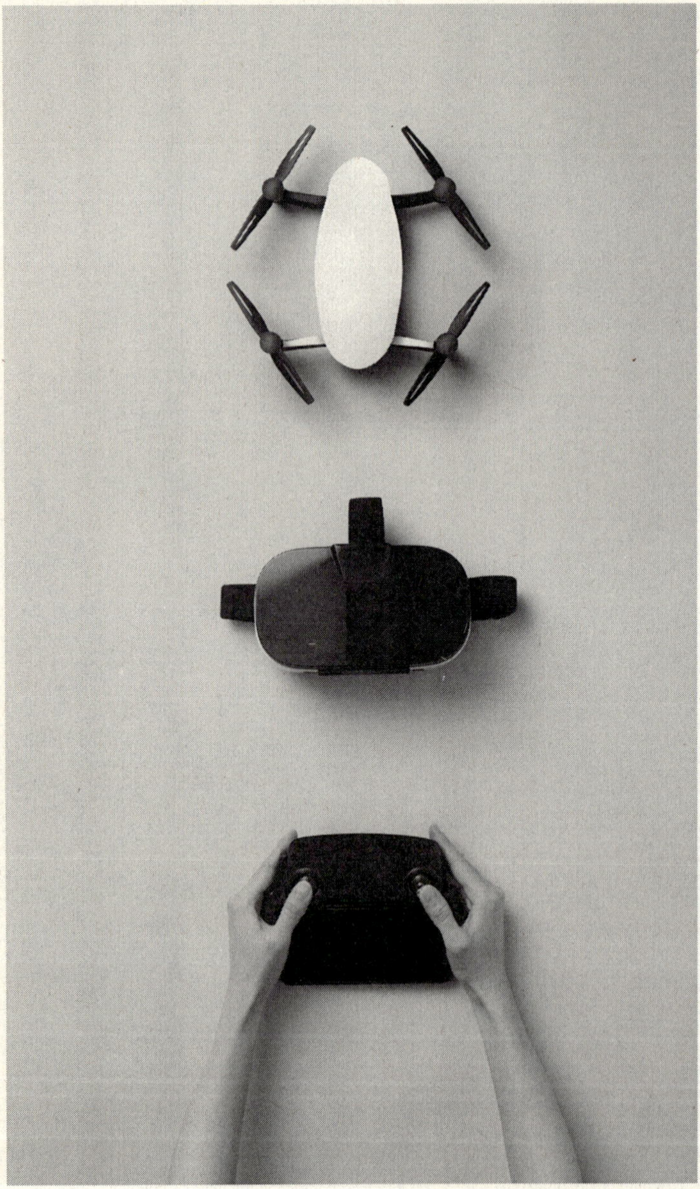

In June 1982, the Israel Defense Forces (IDF) prepared to send thousands of soldiers to attack terrorist positions in Lebanon. A key element in the IDF's strategy was the ability to provide air support to ground forces. Planners knew that Syria—Israel's longtime enemy—had installed 19 guided surface-to-air missile (SAM) systems near the scene of the fighting. These weapons posed a serious threat to Israeli aircraft. They had to be eliminated. In what was known as Operation Mole Cricket 19, the IDF used drones to deal with the threat. Drones are remote-controlled unmanned aerial vehicles (UAVs).

On June 9, **decoy** drones tricked the Syrians into activating the **radar** that controlled the missiles. That enabled the IDF to pinpoint missile locations. The Israelis used precision-guided weapons to destroy the radar systems. Without their radar, the SAMs would not work. A drone fitted with a warhead took out one emplacement. As the operation continued, the IDF also used drones for real-time battlefield **surveillance**. One drone was even responsible for a "no-weapons kill." When a Syrian fighter pilot tried to shoot down the drone, he lost control of his aircraft and crashed.

Drones are helpful in providing aerial surveillance in search-and-rescue missions, particularly in remote or dangerous locations.

Taking Flight

The origins of today's drones can be traced back to 1898. Prolific inventor Nikola Tesla developed a form of wireless radio control that could power and maneuver boats from a distance. As he explained in his **patent** application, "The invention which I have described will prove useful in many ways. Vessels or vehicles of any suitable kind may be used ... for many other scientific, engineering, or commercial purposes; but the greatest value of my invention will result from its effect upon warfare and armaments, for by reason of its certain and unlimited destructiveness it will tend to bring about and maintain permanent peace among nations."

> **TAKEAWAY**
>
> Some people believe that the term "drone" originated with the DH.82 Queen Bee.

When World War I broke out, though, the United States military tried to adapt radio control to unmanned airplanes. The army and navy worked on aerial torpedoes, which would carry explosives behind enemy lines and crash to detonate them. The first functioning version became known as the "Kettering Bug." It was named for Charles Kettering, an engineer at General Motors who advised the project. Following a successful flight test in 1918, the army placed a large order. Nearly 50 Kettering Bugs were built, but the war ended before any could be used.

After the war, the British developed radio-controlled airplanes that could be used for antiaircraft target practice. One was a version of the de Havilland Tiger Moth. It was called the DH.82 Queen Bee. Some people believe that the term "drone" originated with this aircraft,

Reginald, Ronald, and Norma Jeane

Reginald Denny was a child actor. During World War I, he enlisted in England's Royal Flying Corps. He spent the 1920s as a stunt pilot. An interest in radio-controlled model airplanes led him to start Radioplane Company in the 1930s. Wanting to publicize his company, he asked another actor friend, Ronald Reagan, to arrange for pictures to be taken at his factory. (At the time, Reagan was an army captain who made training films.) Reagan's photographer was impressed by a young factory worker named Norma Jeane Dougherty. Norma Jeane became a model and actress, dyed her hair blonde, and changed her name to Marilyn Monroe.

In addition to the Kettering Bug, Charles Kettering helped to develop the electric cash register, key-operated vehicle ignition, and incubators for premature babies.

because a drone is a male bee whose primary function is to serve the queen. Another possibility is that the low humming sound of the aircraft as it approached enemy gunners could be described as a drone.

It took a British export to fully develop the potential of drones. Reginald Denny was a noted actor who appeared onstage and in dozens of films. He came to the U.S. after the end of World War I. Besides furthering his acting career, Denny became interested in radio-controlled model airplanes. In 1934, he opened a hobby shop and sold model planes. In the late 1930s, he formed the Radioplane Company to develop and manufacture larger versions. Soon, he invented the OQ-2. About 8.5 feet (2.6 m) long, it was used to train antiaircraft gunners. Radioplane eventually sold more than 15,000 of these targets to the U.S. Army, making the OQ-2s the first mass-produced drones.

The need for UAVs to carry out **reconnaissance** missions was high during the **Cold War**. One of the first was the Ryan Firebee I. It could stay aloft for nearly 2 hours and soar as high as 60,000 feet (18,288 m). Drones such as the jet-powered Ryan Model 147 Lightning Bug were used extensively during the Vietnam

War. The UAVs carried out missions that would have been extremely dangerous for manned aircraft.

During the 1970s and '80s, the U.S. and Israel were the nations most active in developing drone technology. Drones played an important role for Israel in the 1982 Lebanon War. The U.S. used drones during the 1990–91 Persian Gulf War. During one mission, terrified Iraqi soldiers waved sheets and white shirts at the UAV. It marked the first time enemy troops surrendered to a drone.

In 1995, the General Atomics MQ-1 Predator entered service. It is perhaps the best-known military drone. It is 27 feet (8.2 m) long, and its thin wings extend 49 feet (14.9 m). Because the Predator is much lighter than piloted aircraft, it can stay aloft for more than 24 hours. An engine similar to those used on snowmobiles drives a propeller mounted at the rear. A **bulbous** nose contains its control system. A small camera pod is mounted under the nose. The Predator's cameras are so powerful that they can focus on an individual's face from 25,000 feet (7,620 m). Upside-down, V-shaped fins just in front of the propeller help maintain inflight stability.

The Predator flies high enough that no one on the ground can hear it. Unlike satellites, which provide momentary glimpses of Earth as they continue on their orbital path, Predators can remain in position for hours. Already lighter than manned aircraft of their size, Predators do not carry the additional weight of a pilot and support systems. The drones also do not need to land for food or rest. And if clouds obscure their objectives, the drones can dip below to provide ongoing surveillance.

In 2007, the General Atomics MQ-9 Reaper became operational and began to replace Predators. The Reaper is longer than the Predator. Its wingspan stretches 66 feet (20.1 m). The engine is much more powerful, allowing the drone to cruise nearly twice as fast as its predecessor. Both the Predator and the Reaper are controlled from

TAKEAWAY

The Reaper is longer than the Predator. Its wingspan stretches 66 feet (20.1 m).

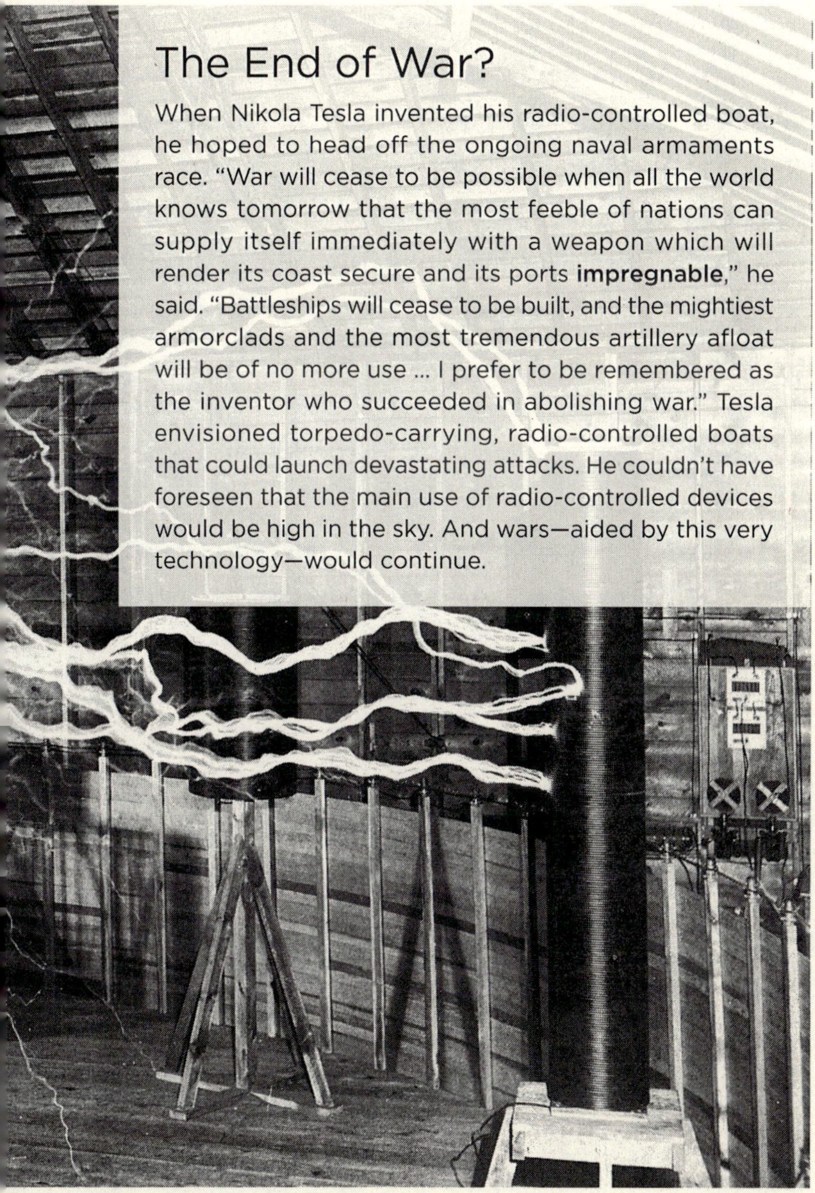

The End of War?

When Nikola Tesla invented his radio-controlled boat, he hoped to head off the ongoing naval armaments race. "War will cease to be possible when all the world knows tomorrow that the most feeble of nations can supply itself immediately with a weapon which will render its coast secure and its ports **impregnable**," he said. "Battleships will cease to be built, and the mightiest armorclads and the most tremendous artillery afloat will be of no more use ... I prefer to be remembered as the inventor who succeeded in abolishing war." Tesla envisioned torpedo-carrying, radio-controlled boats that could launch devastating attacks. He couldn't have foreseen that the main use of radio-controlled devices would be high in the sky. And wars—aided by this very technology—would continue.

remote stations. These stations are often thousands of miles away from the operational zone. The two crew members wear flight suits and sit in large padded seats. As one pilot explained, "You do actually fly it. You can put it on autopilot, but you do have a joystick, you have throttle, you have all that, so you do fly the aircraft." The crew is part of what is known as a remote-split operation. For efficiency reasons, the air force established several stations in the U.S. that use a combination of undersea fiber-optic cables and satellites to control the drones. This arrangement has a huge benefit for the drone crews. Since missions may last longer than a conventional 8- or 12-hour shift, the crews simply turn over the operation to the next shift. Then they go home to their families.

Such a remote system has at least one drawback, though. Even with almost instantaneous communication between crew and drone, it can take up to 1.5 seconds for the signal to reach the drone. This has minimal effect when the aircraft is aloft. But it can be dangerous for takeoff and landing. So crews in closer proximity to the drone base control those aspects of the flight.

The U.S. military has an estimated 11,000 drones, the majority of which are AeroVironment RQ-11 Ravens.

The small Raven resembles a model airplane with nose-mounted cameras. Soldiers in the field launch the Raven by simply throwing it forward. Once airborne, it can fly up to 6 miles (9.7 km) while remaining aloft for as long as 90 minutes. Its portability and ease of operation allow for its immediate deployment when battlefield commanders need prompt intelligence or surveillance.

The model-sized RQ-11 Raven is launched into the air by hand, transmits video in color and infrared imagery, and lands itself.

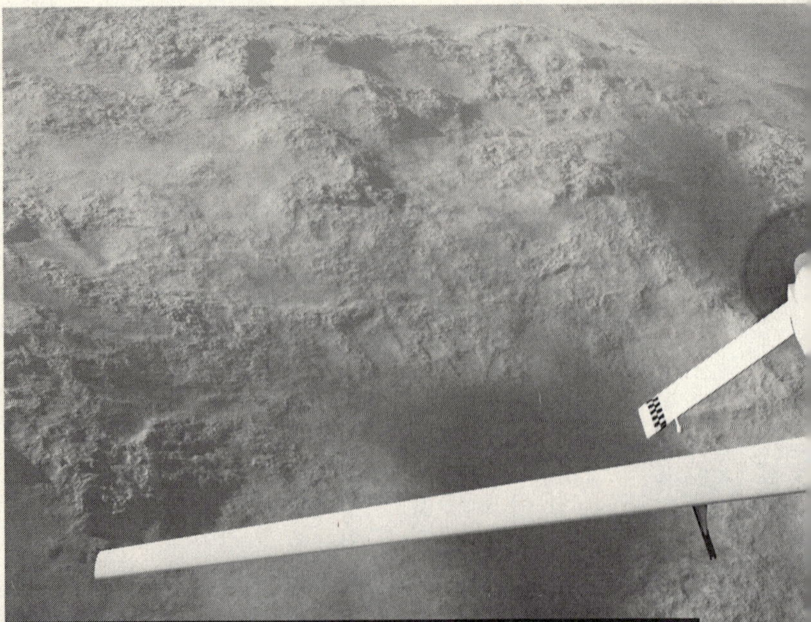

Exploding Balloons

The first use of UAVs in warfare occurred in 1849. At that time, Austria controlled Venice. To crush a Venetian revolt, Austria launched dozens of unmanned balloons carrying explosives over the city. The wind blew in the wrong direction and carried some of the balloons back over Austrian forces. For the defenders, it was a source of entertainment. "Venetians, abandoning their homes, crowded into the streets and squares to enjoy the strange spectacle," wrote an eyewitness. "When a cloud of smoke appeared in the air to make an explosion, all clapped and shouted. Applause was greatest when the balloons blew over the Austrian forces and exploded." The Austrians tried again a month later. The result was much the same. But the Venetians surrendered two days later.

Airborne Snipers

Using an aircraft carrier as a mobile base of operations, military drones can monitor vast areas of the ocean.

On October 12, 2000, the American guided-missile destroyer USS *Cole* lay at anchor in the port city of Aden, Yemen. Shortly before noon, crew members began lining up for lunch. But they never had a chance to eat. A small boat carrying two men and hundreds of pounds' worth of explosives rammed the vessel. The resulting explosion blew a massive hole in the side of the ship. Seventeen sailors were killed, and 39 others were injured. The ship was so badly damaged that it had to be placed on a larger ship and returned to the U.S. Months of work were required to repair the *Cole*.

In a 2013 documentary, several drone experts, including Abraham Karem (right), discussed the future political and ethical challenges posed by drones.

The Dronefather

Abraham Karem was born in Iraq in 1937. As a youngster, he took apart a radio to "see where is the man who talks from there." His family moved to Israel in 1952. In 1974, he started his own company to work on drones for the IDF. But the IDF didn't like any of his designs. Karem moved to the U.S. three years later, in hopes of securing greater opportunities. American-made drones were not reliable. For years, Karem worked out of his garage. The culmination of his efforts was the Predator drone. "I just wanted UAVs to perform to the same standards of safety, reliability, and performance as manned aircraft," he said. Many people call Karem "The Dronefather" for his innovative designs.

The terrorist organization al Qaeda claimed responsibility for the blast. U.S. intelligence sources eventually identified Qaed Salim Sinan al-Harethi, a high-ranking member of al Qaeda, as being involved in the attack. American forces sought to locate him. Predator drones played an important part in the search. But brief sightings turned to frustration as he quickly vanished. On November 3, 2002, al-Harethi was positively identified as one of seven men in an SUV driving along an isolated road in Yemen. High overhead, a Predator drone armed with laser-guided Hellfire missiles kept track of the vehicle. After receiving approval from the Yemeni government, senior officials in the administration of U.S. president George W. Bush gave the order to fire. Moments later, a missile slammed into the SUV, killing al-Harethi and five other men. The seventh was badly wounded.

Up to that point, Predators had been used only for reconnaissance. But with the onset of the War on Terror after the September 11, 2001, attacks in America, the UAVs were equipped with missiles. Some people in law enforcement believed that by pinpointing al-Harethi's location, the military could have captured him and put him on trial. Others had the opposite reaction, arguing

Newer versions of the Predator drone could carry up to four 100-pound (45.4 kg) Hellfire missiles at a time.

White House Red Alert

Around 3:00 a.m. on January 26, 2015, a man decided to fly a drone from the window of his Washington, D.C., apartment, even though doing so was against federal law. He lost control of the drone. It headed for the White House. Only two feet (0.6 m) in diameter, the drone didn't appear on the White House radar system, which is designed to detect objects such as airplanes and missiles. A Secret Service officer noticed the drone and raised the alarm. But he couldn't bring down the UAV. Moments later, it crashed into a tree on the South Lawn. Although the drone itself didn't pose a direct threat to president Barack Obama or his family, its flight pointed to the potential dangers a drone could constitute in the future.

> **TAKEAWAY**
>
> Since the al-Harethi operation, hundreds of drone strikes have been carried out. Most remain shrouded in secrecy.

that when at war, it becomes necessary to use all available weapons to defeat the enemy.

Since the al-Harethi operation, hundreds of drone strikes have been carried out. Most remain shrouded in secrecy. There is a belief that these airstrikes are surgical, or capable of pinpointing their target. Some people see them as a kind of "push-button war," almost like a video game. Although drones have killed several known terrorists, sometimes the intended targets aren't the only victims. Civilians in the vicinity of the strike can also be killed. Despite the precision of these attacks, mistakes can be made. In 2013, a convoy was identified as carrying terrorists. In reality, it was a wedding procession. Fifteen people with no terrorist ties were killed by the airstrike. On another occasion, a missile had just been launched toward a house. A small boy playing nearby had no idea of the approaching danger. He ran into the house a moment before the missile struck. "The night you choose to strike, it may be that the in-laws arrived earlier in the day or the children's birthday party is ongoing and you weren't watching when everyone arrived," said a retired air force colonel. "You never ever have perfect information."

There can also be issues with clarity. Even a slight amount of fuzziness can suggest that a man trudging along with a walking stick might appear to be armed with a rifle. Faces can dissolve into meaningless blobs. "On good days, when a host of environmental, human, and technological factors came together, we had a strong sense that who we were looking at was the person we were looking for," said a former drone pilot. "On bad days, we were literally guessing." It's not clear how many civilians have been killed by drone strikes. According to the London-based Bureau of Investigative Journalism, more than 1,500 noncombatants have died since the early 2000s. Official U.S. government figures are far lower.

TAKEAWAY

More than 1,500 noncombatants have died since the early 2000s. Official U.S. government figures are far lower.

The impersonal nature of drone strikes can serve as a recruiting tool for terrorist organizations such as al Qaeda. In 2011, a report by the United Kingdom's Ministry of Defense said that the use of drones "enables the **insurgent** to cast himself in the role of underdog and the West as a cowardly bully—that is unwilling to risk his own troops, but is happy to kill remotely."

Drone pilots are in a unique position. They are thousands of miles from their targets. That spares them from the intensity and danger of close combat, in which the enemy can fire back. This absence of danger can erode the warrior ethic. (That is the belief that people in combat must assume some measure of risk.) As a result, some pilots report feelings of guilt and remorse. Furthermore, their drones remain overhead when the attack is over to assess the outcome of the strike. Seeing those results can be upsetting, especially when things do not go according to plan. Pilots of manned aircraft rarely see the aftermath of their strikes.

For drone pilots, returning home to their families at the end of a shift is beneficial. But there is a hitch. Pilots are often on edge, especially if they have fired missiles and observed the consequences of their attack yet are not allowed to reveal details of their missions. "In a deployed location, when you are in a traditional aircraft, there is time to **decompress** before you finally get back home," said a pilot. "The Air Force has done a very good job, though, in giving us a plethora [abundance] of resources to talk to and work with … and different techniques for de-stressing." Despite such drawbacks, two things seem certain: Targeted drone strikes will continue, and they will remain controversial.

Army drone operators are trained on UAVs such as the MQ-1C Gray Eagle, RQ-7 Shadow, and RQ-11 Raven.

Civilian Drones

People operating personal drones must follow federal safety rules, including flying the drone lower than 400 feet (122 m), keeping it in sight, and steering it away from other aircraft.

Of course, military forces aren't the only ones using drones. In recent years, drone sales have exploded in the civilian marketplace. It's now possible to buy a drone for less than $100. The Federal Aviation Administration (FAA), which regulates all matters related to air and space in the U.S., calls these civilian forms "unmanned aircraft systems" (UAS). Fixed-wing drones such as the Predator, Reaper, and Global Hawk use the same principles of flight as manned airplanes. As they move forward, the shape of the wing—curved on top, flat on the bottom—reduces air pressure on top of the wing. When these drones achieve a certain speed along the runway, the higher pressure on the underside of the wing pushes the aircraft upward. Most civilian drones, on the other hand, are based on the same principles of flight as helicopters. Nearly all helicopters have two, three, or four rotor blades. The blades are shaped like thin wings and attached to a hub in the center. As the hub spins, the air flows more slowly on top of the rotors than on the bottom. This creates lift. The helicopter takes off by going straight up. A much smaller rotor system mounted on the tail provides stability.

Many drones operate similarly to helicopters, with one important difference: Drones are multicopters. They have more than two rotors. Each rotor has its own

TAKEAWAY

Multicopters have an even number of blades. Half of the blades rotate clockwise, while the other blades rotate counterclockwise.

motor, which is powered by a rechargeable battery. Multicopters have an even number of blades. Half of the blades rotate clockwise, while the other blades rotate counterclockwise. These opposing rotations cancel out the **torque** that would otherwise cause the drone to spin out of control. The most common multicopter is the quadcopter. It has four rotors. Generally, the larger the drone, the more powerful the motors must be. The additional weight may require more rotors to support it. The size of these drones can vary considerably. The Wallet Drone is just 1.6 inches (4.1 cm) wide. Others measure several feet in width.

To move forward, the drone's rearmost rotors must spin faster. That drops the front. The opposite is true to move backward. When all rotors spin at the same speed, the drone can hover, or remain motionless. There are two ways to control a multicopter drone in flight. One is with a handheld remote-control device. It transmits commands directly to the drone. The other is **autonomous** flight, using a computer, tablet, or mobile phone program to preplan the drone's path.

Operators should become completely familiar with their drone at home before taking it out for a spin. There

UFOs and Drones

On the evening of October 16, 2018, dozens of people called a New Jersey television station. They claimed to have seen an unidentified flying object (UFO). One person posted a video on their Twitter feed. It showed an object with flashing red-and-white lights. The "UFO" was simply a police drone. It was aiding the search for two men who had robbed a nearby Home Depot store. As UAV usage has grown, many people are reporting UFO sightings that turn out to be drones. In some cases, the confusion is understandable. The shape of many drones resembles the classic circular structure often associated with UFOs.

are important safety rules to follow as well. The drone cannot fly higher than 400 feet (122 m). Operators must keep the craft in sight at all times. Drones are not allowed to fly near airports, moving vehicles, or places such as athletic stadiums where large numbers of people are present. These devices should also be kept away from private property, as out-of-control drones could damage homes or landscaping. More importantly, many people are concerned about drones—and drone pilots—intruding on their privacy.

Almost from the beginning, drones have been equipped to carry cameras. A **gimbal** holds the camera steady despite vibrations caused by the spinning rotors. The resulting crystal-clear photos and videos add a new and exciting dimension to recreational activities and events.

Drone operators also need to use common sense and discretion. In a video posted to YouTube in mid-November 2018, drone footage showed a mother bear and her cub struggling to climb a steep wall of snow. Many viewers commented on the cub's determination to reach the top after his mother successfully arrived there. The cub slid down twice. On its third attempt, it made good progress. But the operator flew his drone closer.

Because of the noise it made and its proximity to her cub, the mother bear regarded it as a threat. She took a swing at the drone. That startled the cub. It also knocked away some of the snow the young bear was using for traction. The cub tumbled all the way to the bottom of the slope. Perhaps sensing his mistake, the operator backed his drone away. The cub finally clambered all the way back up to the top. Mother and cub loped away, suggesting that the drone was still upsetting them. "The cub could've been killed in the fall," said a wildlife expert. "Beyond that, having to climb all the way back up that slope was a tremendous energy expenditure for such a small cub, which could jeopardize its survival."

Drones reached a significant milestone in 2014 when the FAA approved their use on movie and television sets. Prior to that, movies such as the James Bond film *Skyfall*, the Harry Potter series, and *Transformers* were filmed overseas using drones. The 2014 ruling allowed filmmakers to use them domestically as well. In many cases, drones replaced more-dangerous helicopters. Between 1980 and 2014, 33 people were killed in film-related helicopter accidents. In addition to being safer, drones are cheaper to operate. And, because of their smaller size, they can get closer to the action.

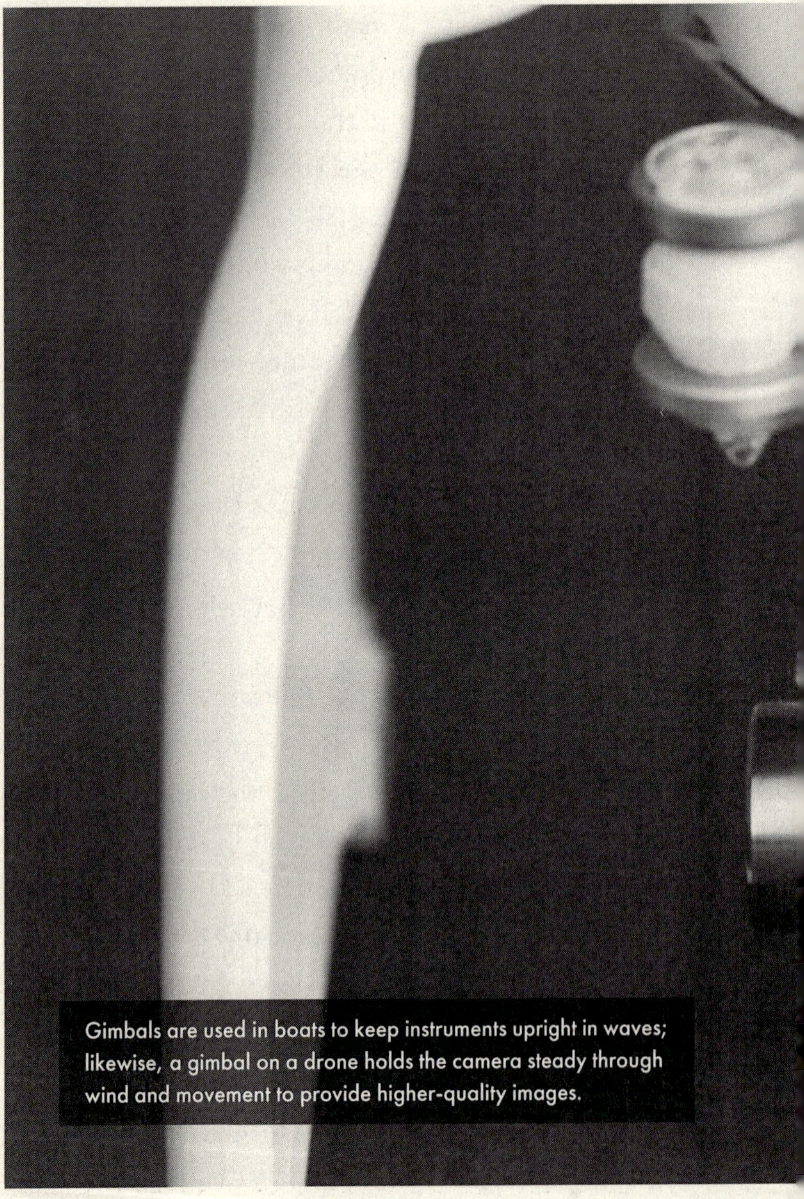

Gimbals are used in boats to keep instruments upright in waves; likewise, a gimbal on a drone holds the camera steady through wind and movement to provide higher-quality images.

Commercial filmmaking is just one of many uses for drones. Drones can monitor shark activity at beaches. They can fly over areas that might be dangerous for manned aircraft, such as erupting volcanoes. Even if something happens to the drone, no person is at risk. Some farmers use drones to herd animals such as sheep and cattle. The devices can also locate these animals in remote pastures much faster than dogs or people. The restaurant chain YO! Sushi has one of the more unusual uses. In 2013, the London-based restaurant introduced iTray, a small drone that delivers meals to customers' tables. Waitstaff use iPads to oversee the operation, and two small cameras help avoid midair collisions.

A more recent development is drone racing. In these competitions, drones often fly out of the pilot's direct line of sight. The drones' cameras stream video back to the pilot, who wears special goggles to see where the drone is going. Using these first-person view (FPV) goggles, the pilot can maneuver the drone around obstacles that appear in its path at speeds approaching 80 miles (129 km) an hour. To make the action easier to watch, many racing drones have special lights illuminating their paths.

Some races are time trials. In these, drones race one at a time. The one with the fastest time wins. Other races have several drones flying at the same time. The presence of multiple drones adds to the split-second decisions the pilot must make. Like cars, drones also have drag races. They line up two-by-two, motionless, and then accelerate toward the finish line. There are many drone-racing clubs throughout the country. The Drone Sports Association (DSA) oversees the U.S. National Drone Racing Championships and the World Drone Racing Championships. The Drone Racing League (DRL) stages events in large stadiums. ESPN broadcasts these races for fans.

Outdoor enthusiasts can fit small drones in their backpacks and carry them along to capture scenic pictures while on adventures.

Looking Ahead

Vanuatu comprises a string of more than 80 islands, and most residents live in rural areas far from healthcare clinics and medical supplies.

Recent developments indicate ways in which drones may be used to help people. Several villages in the South Pacific island nation of Vanuatu are largely cut off from the outside world. Few have paved roads or electricity. As a result, many children do not receive important vaccinations. At the end of 2018, Vanuatu became the first country to adopt an official drone-dependent childhood vaccination program. An Australian startup company called Swoop Aero demonstrated that its fixed-wing autonomous drones could fly more than 30 miles (48.3 km) and land within a 6-foot (1.8 m) circle. The small payload contains

Zipline drones from California deliver up to one ton (907 kg) of medicine and blood products each day in African nations such as Rwanda and Ghana.

vaccines cooled by ice packs.

This isn't the only example of drones being used to convey vital health-related services. In 2016, California-based Zipline International began delivering medical supplies, including blood for transfusions, to a network of clinics and hospitals in the African country of Rwanda. "Rwanda has a vision to become a technology hub for East Africa and ultimately the whole continent of Africa," said Zipline cofounder William Hetzler. "Projects like ours fit very well with that strategy."

Another startup company, called Lift Aircraft, offers short, scenic flights in its 18-rotor Hexa ultralight drone. Beginning operations in 2019, the fledgling Texas company hopes to eventually expand to more than two dozen cities. "We believe the aspiration to fly is wired into the human brain, so don't believe [this is] a novelty," said Lift's chief executive officer Matt Chasen. "We want to deliver a safe, simple flying experience so that anyone can experience the thrill and magic of flying." Those wishing to fly go through an orientation and up to an hour of virtual reality training before venturing out. Chasen compares the flights to a video game in terms of the ability to control the flight, using a joystick and touchscreen display. Remote safety pilots monitor each flight. In case of emergency, they take over and land the Hexa.

Lift Aircraft isn't the only company interested in passenger drones. Several companies are working on autonomous and human-piloted drone taxis. These taxis would enable people to bypass congested highways. However, implementing this service would require **infrastructure** to accommodate drone takeoffs and landings. It also raises several questions: How much air space would the drones need? How would they interact and avoid collisions with other flying vehicles? These considerations and others are likely to put off full-scale service for several years.

Perhaps no other use for drones is as widely anticipated as Amazon's plans to use a vast fleet of drones. The drones would deliver packages weighing up to 5 pounds (2.3 kg) in as little as 30 minutes. Amazon announced the formation of what will be called Prime Air in late 2013. Three years later, it delivered a package to a British family. Amazon has taken out many patents and continued testing, but the company has many regulatory issues to resolve before it can begin offering the service to customers.

The Biggest Drone

The world's largest surveillance drone, the RQ-4 Global Hawk, is nearly 48 feet (14.6 m) long. Its wingspan stretches 131 feet (39.9 m). The drone's purpose is to provide aerial intelligence, so it doesn't carry weapons. It can stay aloft for more than 30 hours. That enables it to survey up to 40,000 square miles (103,600 sq km)! Because it can fly 60,000 feet (18,288 m) high, it is also used to track and study hurricanes and other storms from above. In April 2001, a Global Hawk flew from Edwards Air Force Base in California to RAAF Base Edinburgh in Australia. It was the first UAV to fly nonstop across the Pacific Ocean. The total distance of the roughly 23-hour flight was about 8,600 miles (13,840 km).

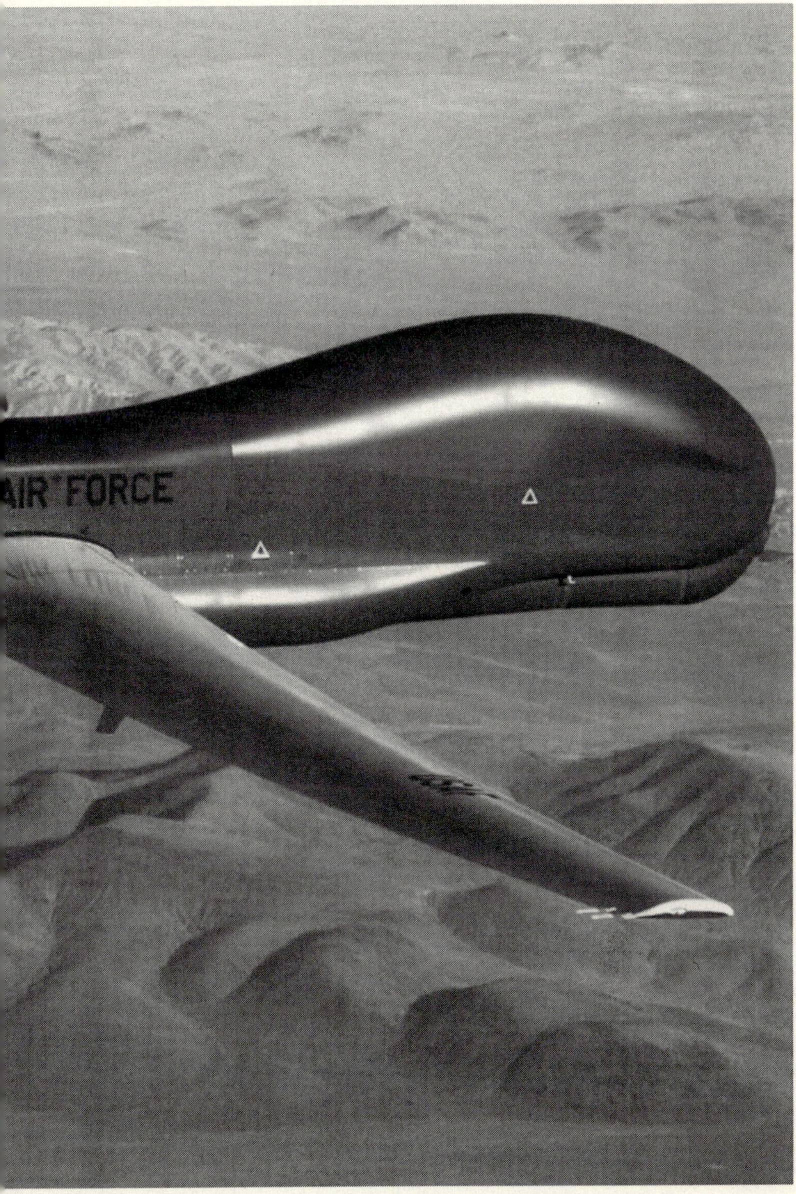
AIR FORCE

TAKEAWAY

Government estimates indicate that at least 100,000 drone-related jobs will be added to the workforce by 2025.

With so many exciting current and future uses for drones, it clearly is a fast-growing field that offers plenty of employment opportunities. Government estimates indicate that at least 100,000 drone-related jobs will be added to the workforce by 2025. The basic requirement to take advantage of these opportunities is a Remote Pilot Certificate, which is available through the FAA. To qualify, one must be at least 16; able to speak, write, and understand English; in reasonable physical condition; clear a background check; and pass an FAA knowledge exam. The exam includes subjects such as drone regulations, preflight maintenance procedures, and the effect of weather on drone performance. This exam must be taken every other year to maintain certification.

One career option involves building a drone business from the ground up. This requires tremendous dedication and commitment, at least a basic knowledge of business and accounting practices, and exceptional flying skills. Even so, as the price for high-quality, commercial-grade drones has dropped to as little as $1,000 in recent years, the UAVs are being implemented in a variety of fields. Real estate agents are turning to drones for their imagery capabilities. Drone footage can show not only the house itself but also its surroundings in a way that ground-level photography cannot. Pilots provide a combination of still photos and video that presents the house's best features and may help capture a quick sale.

Another area where drones are becoming increasingly popular is infrastructure inspection. This dangerous job becomes risk-free with drones. They can detect tiny imperfections that could develop into major problems if not fixed. Insurance companies often call upon drones to survey damage after natural disasters. Farming and agriculture provide numerous occasions to utilize drones. So do fields like transportation, energy, education, public safety, and many others.

The armed forces offer another route to employment.

By January 2018, more than one million drones—including 878,000 for hobbyists and 122,000 commercial, public, and others—were registered with the FAA.

Every branch of the American military includes UAV pilot positions, though requirements vary. Initially, the air force only used officers trained in flying manned aircraft to operate drones. As the number of drones increased, the organization began training officers specifically to fly them. The air force also has begun recruiting enlisted personnel to pilot the Global Hawk. The first operators received their wings in 2017 after a seven-month training program. According to official air force estimates, about 70 percent of Global Hawk pilots eventually will be enlisted members.

The army has already welcomed enlisted personnel as drone pilots. Their official title is Unmanned Aerial Systems Operators. Potential operators must have a high school diploma. They need to score 102 or higher on the Surveillance and Communications area of the Armed Services Vocational Aptitude Battery (ASVAB). They must be a U.S. citizen, obtain a secret security clearance, possess normal color vision, and have a clean record. Training begins with 10 weeks of basic combat training. That's followed by 23 weeks of advanced individual training, a combination of classroom and hands-on learning.

TAKEAWAY

Insurance companies often call upon drones to survey damage after natural disasters.

Whether they are in the military, working one of the multitudes of civilian jobs, or simply enjoying a hobby, the number of drone pilots is sure to increase in the coming years. Drones will become even more affordable and continue to offer exciting new possibilities as their popularity and presence grows.

NO DRONE
ZONE

A Downside to Drones

A few days before Christmas in 2018, someone deliberately flew a drone into the airspace of London's Gatwick Airport. Officials had to shut down the airport while police searched for the operator. "Each time we believe we get close to the operator, the drone disappears; when we look to reopen the airfield, the drone reappears," said one officer. Two suspects were arrested and quickly released. Thousands of people were stuck at Gatwick. Thousands more were stranded when flights were canceled and planes were forced to land as far away as Paris. Gatwick had briefly closed the previous year because of a drone sighting. Authorities expressed concern that incidents such as this could occur more frequently.

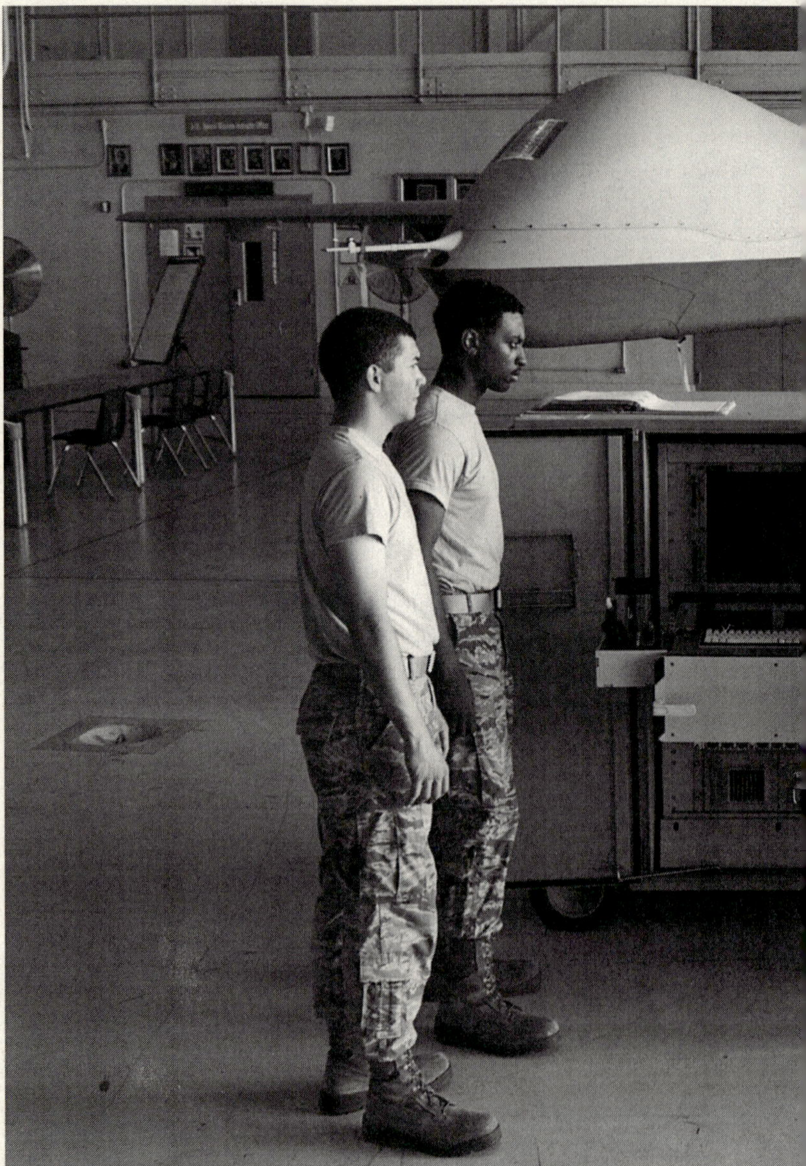

Unmanned aircraft systems repair personnel in the army maintain drones and make sure the UAVs are fully equipped to conduct their missions.

Timeline

1849	Austria attacks Venice using unmanned balloons carrying explosives.
1898	Nikola Tesla demonstrates his radio-controlled boat at Madison Square Garden.
1918	The U.S. military develops the pilotless Kettering Bug, but World War I ends before the UAVs can be used.
1941	Radioplane Company begins delivering OQ-2 target drones to the air force and eventually produces about 15,000 units for the military.
1977	Abraham Karem moves from Israel to the U.S.; within a decade, he develops an early version of the Predator drone.
1982	IDF uses drones to destroy Syrian air defense systems in Lebanon.
1995	The Predator drone enters service as a surveillance tool.
1998	The Global Hawk drone makes its first flight. Three years later, it becomes the first UAV to cross the Pacific Ocean.
2002	A Predator carries out the first targeted UAV killing of a terrorist leader.

2006	The FAA authorizes the use of drones in civilian airspace and begins issuing commercial drone permits.
2007	The Reaper drone makes its first combat flight.
2010	The Parrot AR becomes the first consumer quadcopter drone controlled by smartphone.
2013	Amazon announces plans to make home deliveries using drones.
2014	The FAA permits drone use for movie and TV production companies.
2015	A small drone crosses the White House fence undetected and crashes on the South Lawn.
2016	Amazon delivers a package to a home in England within 30 minutes of order placement.
2018	The air force completes its phaseout of Predator drones.

Selected Bibliography

Aitken, Paul, Rob Burdick, and Tim Ray. *Livin' the Drone Life: An Insider's Guide to Flying Drones for Fun and Profit*. Austin, Tex.: Lioncrest, 2016.

Arkin, William M. *Unmanned: Drones, Data, and the Illusion of Perfect Warfare*. New York: Little, Brown and Company, 2015.

Cheng, Eric. Aerial Photography and *Videography Using Drones*. San Francisco: Peachpit Press, 2015.

Fuller, S. L. "A Day in the Life of a U.S. Air Force Drone Pilot." *Aviation Today*, March 16, 2017. https://www.aviationtoday.com/2017/03/16/day-life-us-air-force-drone-pilot/.

Juniper, Adam. The *Complete Guide to Drones*. 2nd ed. New York: Wellfleet Press, 2018.

Press, Eyal. "The Wounds of the Drone Warrior." *New York Times Magazine*, June 13, 2018. https://www.nytimes.com/2018/06/13/magazine/veterans-ptsd-drone-warrior-wounds.html.

Woods, Chris. Sudden Justice: *America's Secret Drone Wars*. New York: Oxford University Press, 2015.

Zaloga, Steven J. *Unmanned Aerial Vehicles: Robotic Air Warfare*, 1917–2007. New York: Osprey, 2008.

Glossary

autonomous	undertaken without outside control; self-contained or independent
bulbous	resembling a bulb; rounded or swollen
Cold War	a period of hostile rivalry after World War II between the communist Soviet Union and the democratic United States
decompress	relieve or reduce pressure or stress
decoy	something used to lead someone or something into a trap or to draw attention away from a threat
gimbal	a mechanism used to keep an instrument steady
impregnable	unable to be captured or broken into
infrastructure	structures such as bridges, roadways, or power grids necessary for the operation of a system, activity, or organization
insurgent	a person who revolts against an established government; a rebel
patent	an official document guaranteeing the exclusive right to create, use, or sell an invention for a set period of time
radar	a system used to detect objects such as aircraft and determine their position and velocity
reconnaissance	exploratory military observation of an enemy to obtain information
surveillance	close watch kept over someone or something
torque	a force that produces a turning or twisting motion

Websites

Drone Racing League

https://thedroneracingleague.com/

Learn about the latest drone developments, watch videos of drone races, and more.

UAV Coach

https://uavcoach.com/uav-jobs/#guide

Read about the different types of work being done with drones.

Note: Every effort has been made to ensure that any websites listed above were active at the time of publication. However, because of the nature of the Internet, it is impossible to guarantee that these sites will remain active indefinitely or that their contents will not be altered.

Index

JAICO PUBLISHING HOUSE

Elevate Your Life. Transform Your World.

ESTABLISHED IN 1946, Jaico Publishing House is home to world-transforming authors such as Sri Sri Paramahansa Yogananda, Osho, the Dalai Lama, Sri Sri Ravi Shankar, Sadhguru, Robin Sharma, Deepak Chopra, Jack Canfield, Eknath Easwaran, Devdutt Pattanaik, Khushwant Singh, John Maxwell, Brian Tracy, and Stephen Hawking.

Our late founder Mr. Jaman Shah first established Jaico as a book distribution company. Sensing that independence was around the corner, he aptly named his company Jaico ('Jai' means victory in Hindi). In order to service the significant demand for affordable books in a developing nation, Mr. Shah initiated Jaico's own publications. Jaico was India's first publisher of paperback books in the English language.

While self-help, religion and philosophy, mind/body/spirit, and business titles form the cornerstone of our non-fiction list, we publish an exciting range of travel, current affairs, biography, and popular science books as well. Our renewed focus on popular fiction is evident in our new titles by a host of fresh young talent from India and abroad. Jaico's recently established translations division translates selected English content into nine regional languages.

Jaico distributes its own titles. With its headquarters in Mumbai, Jaico has branches in Ahmedabad, Bangalore, Chennai, Delhi, Hyderabad, and Kolkata.

SINCE 1946